Getting into the literary world is like an initiation into a secret society. Thank you for helping me break down the barriers to get to the next level.

ALICIA G.

This material has been extremely helpful for me—a total newbie in the publishing world.

BARBARA I.

I am excited and uplifted with fresh confidence this will be the foundation that carries my proposed book projects!

JOHNI

I have been writing for well over thirty years, both for the traditional markets and others. These five days have been most helpful in letting me know that I've been doing many things right and that I need to hone others.

PHYLLIS C.

Thanks for all the enlightening information. This process sounds intimidating, and I appreciate the humor and encouragement! The Pro Tips are also great.

RENEE

What an education I just received! Everything you mentioned is so necessary and needed for developing a selling book proposal. Your Pro Tips are the greatest. What a treasure!

VERA S.

You have equipped me and boosted my confidence exponentially.

SUSAN M.

COMPLETE YOUR BOOK
PROPOSAL IN 5 DAYS

COMPLETE YOUR BOOK PROPOSAL IN 5 DAYS

Your Path to Successful
Book Publishing Starts Here!

Paul Mikos
Director of Author Gateway

Complete Your Book Proposal in 5 Days

Your Path to Successful Book Publishing Starts Here!

Published in Nashville, Tennessee, by Elm Hill, an imprint of Thomas
Nelson. Elm Hill and Thomas Nelson are registered trademarks of
HarperCollins Christian Publishing, Inc.

Elm Hill titles may be purchased in bulk for educational, business,
fund-raising, or sales promotional use. For information, please e-mail
SpecialMarkets@ThomasNelson.com.

For more information, contact Author Gateway,
http://www.authorgateway.com.

Library of Congress Cataloging-in-Publication Data

Library of Congress Control Number: 2019932224

ISBN 978-1-400325061 (Paperback)
ISBN 978-1-400325078 (eBook)

Contents

INTRODUCTION

"Almost every client on my roster completed and submitted a book proposal before I started working with them. In fact, the quality of their proposals was often why they eventually became not only clients, but officially signed authors."

Literary agent Jana Burson,
The Christopher Ferebee Agency

What is the most important tool you need on the journey to becoming a successful author? A pen? A laptop? A good thesaurus? A polished manuscript? Actually, the most important item in the author's toolbox is a quality book proposal. Without it, a writer has almost no hope of attracting the attention of a traditional publisher. Yet shockingly, this critical implement is treated as an afterthought by many unpublished authors who then wonder why they receive rejection after rejection despite all the effort they've put into writing a book.

When professionally prepared, a good book proposal communicates to the industry that you know what it takes to write, publish, market, and sell a book. Whether you've written your first book or your tenth, you need to make sure that your proposal stands out from the crowd and the shines the best light possible on your manuscript.

Forget Your Manuscript (For Now)

Even if you've written a book that will change the life of every person who reads it, it's your book proposal that is the key to opening doors with literary agents, acquisitions editors, publishing boards, booksellers, and even the media. Agents and editors receive thousands of submissions, and very few of these industry professionals will have time to read *any* of your manuscript, so your proposal must do the vital initial work of creating interest in you and your book. Sending a completed manuscript unsolicited—i.e., before it's been requested—is an immediate indicator that you are not a professional and that your manuscript would likely require a lot of extra work to edit, market, and sell.

Pro Tip:

Receiving an unsolicited ream of paper in the mail triggers a reaction among most publishing pros to throw it straight into the recycling bin. Even if your manuscript is complete, follow all submission guidelines and don't send a manuscript until the publisher asks for it.

Spend Time to Save Time

There are nuances to even the simplest information in a book proposal, nuances that telegraph whether the writer is a professional or an amateur. These small details will tell an acquisitions editor either that you've been around the block and are going to be easy to work with, or that you have little knowledge of—or regard for—the art and mechanics of book publishing.

Due to the demands and their time and very real budgetary concerns, publishing pros can manage to read only a limited number of projects each year. If an agent or editor is faced with deciding between two book projects with similar potential, the proposal that requires less work up front has a significant advantage. The time you put into your book proposal will ultimately save time for the people who will work on your behalf in the future, because you've already answered many of their questions. This book is designed to help you focus your time (and your proposal) to save you and others time in the long run.

Why Do I Need to Write a Book Proposal?

Most books considered for publication will have at least two proposals created for them. Under the traditional publishing model, an author looking for representation generally submits a query letter and sample chapters to a literary agent. If they like what they read, the agent then works with the author to develop a strong proposal for submission to acquisitions editors at publishing houses. An acquisitions editor who takes an interest in the book will then develop an in-house version of the proposal to present to a publishing board comprising other editors, a couple of executives, and representatives from marketing, sales, and production. As a team, this publishing board might review dozens of titles in a month to select which books they want to publish.

Your book proposal contains vital information that these publishing professionals need to make an informed choice. An excellent, well-written proposal will make their job easier and make your book much more attractive to them.

Your Business Plan

The good news is that you've been offered a book contract; the bad news is that you can now expect another round of writer's block. At this point in the process, however, it should be called "author's block," because you're likely to get stiff-armed at every turn. Even authors published by major New York houses often find themselves blocked by their own marketing department or publicist and the media. Unless you've spelled out clearly in your proposal what people can do to help market your book, it can be very difficult to motivate them to work creatively on your behalf—even those who are getting paid to do so. This is yet another reason why writing a good book proposal is so important. A professional book proposal is like a business plan in that it's critical to both the birth and the ongoing life of your book.

As with any business plan, a book proposal must be a living document. That means that it needs to be updated regularly to account for recent events—in the world and in your life—and to take advantage of marketing opportunities as they surface. This document, if well researched and well written, is something you and your publisher can return to often for guidance and reminders of your vision.

Tired of Rejection? Do This!

All authors have experienced the pain of rejection. Repeated rejection is simply part of publishing. What many writers fail to realize, however, is that most rejections are caused by poorly researched, poorly written, or poorly constructed book proposals. But it doesn't have to be that way.

In just *five days* you can produce a professional book proposal by working through this booklet. These pages are full of valuable insights from industry professionals and will tell you exactly what they want to see from you. If you will heed their advice, you can feel confident that you are casting your book in the most appealing light possible, thereby giving it the greatest chance of success.

The Book Proposal Template

This booklet is designed to work in tandem with the Author Gateway Book Proposal Template edited by Pete Nikolai, director of Publishing Services at HarperCollins Christian Publishing. You'll want to have that proposal in front of you as you work through this guide.

The Book Proposal Template is a Microsoft Word document, making it user-friendly, approachable, and familiar to most writers. Each section contains a field that you can select and begin entering your own text. This template was developed based on several excellent proposals submitted by agents as well as the in-house proposals used for HarperCollins Christian's publishing board meetings.

The Author Gateway Book Proposal Template is available in the Resources section on our website at www.AuthorGateway.com.

Keep in mind as you work through the template that not every field applies to every author or every book in every genre. For example, biographies, historical novels, gift books, and children's picture books all require somewhat different information in a proposal. Some entries in the template will apply only to nonfiction books. Most of what is included in the Author Gateway Book Proposal Template will apply to your book, but there may be sections you don't use at all.

Now let's get started!

DAY 1

We are going to cover a lot of ground today. Remember, what may seem like tedious details in the book proposal are important telltales that reveal your understanding (or lack thereof) of the publishing industry. Therefore, we are going to walk step-by-step through each section of the book proposal and record crucial data about your book. Along the way you will pick up key insights into traditional publishing that will make you look like a pro.

The final section for Day 1 will deal with the "book hook." This is where you will spend the majority of your time today, and throughout the week you will return to your book hook as you continue to refine your proposal.

The Content

It's time to dive headlong into the first section of your book proposal. At the top of your proposal you will enter the name of the literary agent or publishing house to whom you're submitting the proposal, along with the date of submission. You will want to create a customized proposal for each and every submission.

Titles and Subtitle

Seems easy enough, right? You've been working on your book idea for a while. Perhaps the idea even started with a title. Or maybe you're completely blocked and unable to come up with a single useful idea for your title. In any case, my best advice is this: relax.

It's important to remember that the title you provide in your proposal is a working title only. In fact, you need to consider the whole book to be a work in progress. Should you sign a contract with a traditional publisher, the title will almost certainly be up for discussion among the editorial, marketing, and sales teams. Therefore, it is important that you remain flexible concerning the title, especially during the submission process.

If you're writing a novel, your working title might be the name(s) of one or more characters. Or it might refer to an important theme or a major plot point. For nonfiction books, the title is typically the "big idea," while the subtitle spells out the primary benefit your readers will get from the book. If you haven't been thinking in these terms yet, don't worry. We're going to spend some time later in the process working on articulating the ideas and benefits of your book.

For now, if you don't have a working title in mind, let me suggest that you use WORKING TITLE and WORKING SUBTITLE and revisit them again after you've written more of the proposal. Even if you feel quite confident in your current title, you may want to include the words "working title" in parentheses after the title to communicate your willingness to follow the advice of the experts you're asking to invest in your book.

Author

Enter the name of the author(s), illustrator, and any other contributor to the book exactly as it will appear on the book cover.

Pro Tip:
It's very important to be consistent everywhere you list your name in print. If you plan to include your middle initial on the cover, for example, *always* use your middle initial when marketing and publicizing yourself or your book.

Agent

If you don't yet have an agent but want to pursue one, you can write "TBD" in this section. Write "None" or "N/A" or delete this heading altogether if you have no interest in working with an agent.

Number/Titles of (Other) Books in the Contract

In most cases, signing a separate contract for each of your books is more desirable than a multi-book deal, unless you are proposing a fiction series or children's book series. Otherwise, unrelated books should be proposed individually. You may hear about authors receiving two-book contracts, but it is extremely rare for a new or unknown author to secure a multi-book deal.

In fact, proposing a multi-book contract as a first-time or unknown author can be dangerous. If you've ever watched the television program *Shark Tank,* you've probably seen Mr. Wonderful eviscerate a well-meaning entrepreneur who is eager to share his or her ideas about all the ways their business could grow. Most often, entrepreneurs who are trying to do too much don't get the investments they're seeking because they come across as being easily distracted from the core of their business. Learn from *Shark Tank.* Don't include ideas for additional books unless they are integral to the core concept of the book series you're presenting.

You need to keep the attention of the agent or editor reading your proposal focused on the book at hand and show them that you too are focused. Even if you have a grand vision to expand your book into a series of derivative products, you need to prove the marketability of your core concept first. If you have a realistic vision for your book, others are more likely to catch that vision and want to partner with you in publishing your work.

If you choose to publish independently, you will still need to focus on one concept for your target audience, knowing that you have the freedom to expand on your concepts later for the audience with the most interest and traction.

A WORD ABOUT METADATA

Metadata is industry jargon that you will likely hear in the context of your book. It's one of those technical terms people pretend to understand so they don't look foolish. Simply put, metadata is data about data. In the case of your book proposal, it is data about your book.

Today, metadata is critical for the life and survival of a book. One set of metadata is entered into a publisher's system to be disseminated electronically to distributors and retailers around the world. Once that data is released, changing it is like trying to recapture a bucket of water that's been dumped into a moving stream. If the price of your book changes, it can take days (sometimes weeks) for the correct price to appear on the site of even the most sophisticated online retailer. Therefore, be prepared to temper your frustration during the process. Data systems continue to improve, but metadata changes are inevitable. Getting it right the first time when possible and showing grace for changes in the future will save you a lot of heartache.

BISAC Category

BISAC stands for Book Industry Standards and Communications, and it is managed by the Book Industry Study Group (BISG). BISAC categories help distributors and retailers uniformly categorize books. Visit www.bisg.org to find a current list of these codes.

As you review the BISAC list, you will notice there are specific code numbers attached to each combination of major heading and subheading. In your proposal, list the appropriate code, followed by the headings. Do *not* mix and match major headings or add subheadings.

Pro Tip:
Though you will find other categories and category trees on Amazon and other online book sites, stick to using the BISAC codes only. They are required by distributors and retailers in the metadata templates.

Researching BISAC categories can be fun. It's a good time to imagine exactly where you want your book to appear in the bookstore. The key is to realize that despite how appropriate your book might be in many different sections of the store, you must pick ONE section where the primary target audience is most likely to discover your book. Remember, your book is unlikely to appear on more than one shelf in a brick-and-mortar store. Selecting just one is not an easy decision, but it is critically important that you identify one primary BISAC code. The primary code for this book is:

LAN027000 LANGUAGE ARTS
& DISCIPLINES / Publishing

The great news about online retailing is that your book can appear in multiple categories and may be ranked within each of those categories. Major retailers and distributors have metadata templates that require publishers to enter at least *three* BISAC codes for every title. So you may select up to three codes, but list them in order of accuracy with the primary category at the top of the list. For example, the three codes selected for this book are:

LAN027000 LANGUAGE ARTS
& DISCIPLINES / Publishing

LAN002000 LANGUAGE ARTS
& DISCIPLINES / Authorship

BUS012000 BUSINESS & ECONOMICS
/ Careers / General

Format

Choose hardcover or trade paperback, not both. Hardcovers are reserved for potentially bestselling books. Unless you've previously published a bestseller or you have 50,000 social media followers, go with trade paperback.

Pro Tip:
Use the term "trade paperback" to sound like a pro.

Another important note about the format is to pick only one for your proposal. Again, a bestselling author might launch a book in hardcover, e-book, and audio simultaneously, followed by a trade paperback release some months later. Eventually, there might be a mass-market paperback released for a bestselling novel or a movie tie-in. Do not include these other formats in your proposal. If you are a first-time author, it's best to show some restraint and propose that your book be published as a trade paperback. If a hardcover (or other) release is appropriate for your book, you can be sure that an agent or publisher will make that decision.

If you're publishing independently or working with a hybrid publisher using print-on-demand (POD) inventory management, there's no harm in releasing hardcover and paperback formats simultaneously, thus allowing customers to select their preferred format.

Page Count

To calculate your page count, estimate the total anticipated word count and divide by 250 words per page. Once upon a time, nearly all books were printed on sheet-fed presses in which large sheets of paper were folded and cut into sixteen-page signatures. With digital presses and new binding techniques, the sixteen-page "sig" or eight-page "half-sig" isn't as restrictive anymore, but suggesting a page count that is a multiple of 16 or 8 makes you appear more savvy about publishing.

Pro Tip:

Listing 96 pages, 208 pages, or 304 pages appears more professional than listing 100, 200, or 300 pages.

The listed page count for any book is the total number of actual pages in the book, including the front matter, back matter, and even blank pages. So round your page count up to the nearest sig or half-sig.

One final note: using word count to estimate children's picture books is not especially helpful. But you'll notice that most picture books are 16, 32, or 48 pages in length, so aim for one of those sizes.

Trim Size

The trim size indicates the actual horizontal and vertical dimensions of your book. The most common size for hardcover books is 6 inches x 9 inches, but not every book feels right at that size. Trade paperbacks tend to be about 5 ½ x 8 ½. Some other common sizes include:

- 5 x 8 for more intimate and reflective books
- 5 x 7 or 4 x 6 for a gift book or small booklet
- 4 x 7 is a mass market paperback and is typically not used for a first-run book unless it's a specialty format

Pro Tip:
The horizontal measurement always comes before the vertical measurement when referring to trim size, even for books with a landscape orientation.

Common sizes for children's picture books vary significantly but commonly include 8 x 8, 8 x 10, and 10 x 12. Sizes for specialty books such as coffee-table books, cookbooks, and textbooks also vary. The most important thing to consider for a specialty book is how it will be used by the reader.

Pro Tip:
Hardcover books are measured by their page size, not the board (cover) size, so the case of a hardcover book will be larger than the listed size due to the overhang of the boards.

You will find every trim size under the sun on your bookshelves at home and at the bookstore. I encourage you to pick up several books similar to yours, decide what feels best in your hand, then measure the page size. I also encourage you to look up a chart of common sizes through Ingram Spark at www.ingramspark.com/plan-your-book/print/trim-sizes. Selecting a common size will give you more options for printing and will save money at press time.

Retail Price

The most important thing you can do to determine a proposed retail price is research. What are the retail list prices of the top ten books in each of your three BISAC categories? How do the formats of these bestsellers compare to your format?

Pro Tip:

When pricing a book, it's important to distinguish the list price from the sale price. Amazon and others almost always sell books at a discount. Discount prices are irrelevant to your book proposal. Look strictly at list retail prices.

Rounding down prices is a more common practice than using even numbers. For example, a book is more likely to be priced at $14.99 than $15.00. At one publishing house, all books are priced using .99 until they have a special sale—then those books are listed using .97. There's nothing magic about choosing .99 or .97; this was simply a communication tool that helped the in-house sales team recognize that books with a .97 price had special terms. I suggest you stick with .99.

Pro Tip:

Don't leave a dollar on the table. Some list prices are more common than others. For example, $14.99 is more common than $13.99. $19.99 is more common than $17.99 or $18.99. Go with the greater price if the value is there for the customer.

Don't worry too much about pricing. The final cover price will be eventually decided by the publisher based on many factors. Sale pricing will ultimately be determined by the retailers. Just remember that if your book is priced appropriately according to its format, trim size, page count, and category, the reader's decision to purchase your book will most often be driven by the solution your book offers to their problem (felt need) much more than the price.

Ship Date

A Tuesday release date is an industry standard for major book releases, so you might choose a Tuesday in a given month. A certain mythology has grown around why Tuesdays are common. One theory is that Tuesday is when bestseller lists start counting sales for their weekly updates, though that's unlikely in this era of modern sales tracking.

Realistically, most books don't have a hard release date, also known as a "street date." Generally, bookstores put the books on the shelves when they arrive at the store. Street dates are only for the most anticipated new releases, and retailers who sell a title prior to an enforced street date may incur penalties from the publisher. An example of this are the Harry Potter parties booksellers often host before midnight on the street date of the newest release. But let's face it, most books are not going to have people camping outside stores the night before their street date. As authors, you and I have neither cause to set a hard street date nor the leverage to enforce it.

The single most important factor to consider when suggesting a release date is the retail sales cycle. What are stores promoting that time of year, and does your book have a particular appeal during that season?

- January/February: Inspirational and self-help for the new year; Black History Month (historical, African-American interest); Valentine's Day (gift books)
- March/April/May: Easter, books for mom or dad (Mother's Day, Father's Day); new grads (graduation gifts); patriotic (Memorial Day)
- June/July/August: Beach reads, patriotic, back-to-school
- September/October: Autumn, Halloween
- November/December: Christmas, Hanukkah

If your book has a tie-in to one of these retail cycles, it has a reason to be on the shelf at that time of year. Your book may be a great year-round read, but if you're hoping for special retail consideration, choose a retail season that gives your book a good shot at sell-through (industry jargon for cash register sales).

Pro Tip:
If your best shot to get your book into stores is its tie to a specific holiday, then your release date needs to be six to eight weeks prior to that holiday to allow for seasonal sales.

Have you noticed how quickly and early a store changes its seasonal displays? That only happens with a great deal of planning. Last-minute decisions about Christmas displays are made in July. This is equally true for long-lead media, such as print book reviews or feature stories.

You may be familiar with the long lead times of traditional publishers, who tend to release books twelve to eighteen months after the manuscript is turned in by the author. The reason for this lengthy lead time is largely to take advantage of sales cycles to maximize placement of the book in stores (online or otherwise). Retailers and the media need to know about a book at least six months prior to the release date for planning purposes. Often books are pitched to media with Advance Reading Copies (ARCs) for review purposes. This is part of the staging and marketing of books. It takes months to work through the development of each stage. If you get a book deal with a publisher, be a pro and don't grumble about the long wait for your book's release. It's more than likely in your best interest to be patient.

If you choose to publish independently, you are still competing for shelf space in your local bookstore and local media. There may be more grace at your neighborhood bookstore or weekly newspaper, but they are also planning ahead and you must respect their timelines. Give them plenty of notice before you want your book to appear on the shelf or on the review page.

Book Hook

You're likely familiar with the phrase "elevator pitch." It's the idea that you should have a brief, memorized pitch ready to deliver in the span of an elevator ride. Your book hook must deliver even more punch than an elevator pitch; it must communicate the essence of *why* your book matters in one sentence (maybe two).

If you're like most authors, publishing your book is a dream seemingly always on the brink of becoming reality. Signing a book contract really is exciting, but now comes something most authors find quite challenging, if not offensive: *the idea that your book is a product.*

So much love and creativity goes into writing a book, especially one born out of a dream of being a published author. And like most authors, you want your book to touch as many readers as possible. (Picking up a bit of fame and money would be nice too.) But to reach those readers, you must think in commercial, business terms. As cold as it may seem, commercial viability is the primary quality that separates the books that make it into the traditional publishing machine from those that don't. Most traditional publishers or imprints (the brands within a publishing house) have some unifying focus or mission, but all of them are making an investment to acquire and develop your book, just as one company acquires other smaller companies in order to grow. They must be shrewd in seeking out prospects with the best potential return on investment (ROI).

This is the crux of why your book proposal is so critical to your publishing path. Your book proposal should demonstrate how you are mitigating the risk of failure and promising a good ROI. Having a large public platform—that is, the ability to communicate to a large group of loyal followers—is the surest way to get picked up by a traditional publisher, because the publisher can then safely predict that a large number of fans will buy the book regardless of its content.

What do you do if you don't have a large platform?

Focus. Connect your book to one problem felt by one specific group of people. This may seem counterintuitive because we want to believe that a bigger audience is always better, but it is nearly impossible to rise above the noise of the world when speaking to the masses, or even multiple groups. You begin to offset the risk and lower the barrier to marketplace entry when you demonstrate that your book solves a specific problem for a specific group of people who can be readily identified and reached. This is true whether you pursue traditional publishing, assisted self-publishing, hybrid publishing, or independent publishing. If you don't force yourself to think in these terms, you will be frustrated by continual rejection and confusion regardless of the publishing path you choose.

"People buy things because they read words that make them want to buy things." That quote is taken from the jacket copy of Donald Miller's bestselling book *Building a StoryBrand: Clarify Your Message So Customers Will Listen*. Miller uses the seven universal elements of powerful stories to teach people how to dramatically improve how they connect with customers and grow their businesses. In your case, the customer is the reader. If you can connect with a reader through your book hook, this will be instantly recognized by an agent, acquisitions editor, and booksellers.

According to Miller, these are the seven universal story points all humans respond to: a character (your reader) who has a problem, meets a guide (you) who gives them a plan (your book), calls them to action, helps them avoid failure, and ends in success. Miller's process for working out a business message is the best tool I've found for boiling down a concept to one punchy message. Get the book and read it to help you develop your book hook. If this sounds like a commercial for Miller's book, it is. I truly believe his book can help you.

Later you will spend time identifying the market for your book and planning to reach that market. The work you do now on your book hook will pay off later when addressing these topics in your book proposal. But if you're feeling stuck now, then stop and take a break. The work you do throughout the process of writing your book proposal will be helpful in honing your book hook. You can return to this section at any time to make it better.

Day 1 Homework Assignment

Spend focused time on your book hook today. It will serve you well throughout the proposal-writing process. If you're feeling overwhelmed by everything we covered today, let those feelings go. Just start writing whatever comes into your mind in any field to loosen up your thoughts. You will return to each section throughout this process, so don't feel like you have to nail it the first time. Fill in the fields where you can and leave some blank if you must. Each day throughout the five-day challenge we will cover a little bit less ground, giving you more time to revise and polish your proposal.

Day 2

Congratulations! You made it through Day 1, and you're ready to forge ahead. You've taken in a lot of information about seemingly innocuous details. But as you've learned, these details communicate at a glance to an agent or editor that you are an author who is going to make their job easier, and this increases the likelihood that they'll want to work with you.

On Day 1, you began working on your book hook, boiling down to one or two sentences the book concept that's the foundation of your entire proposal. It's unlikely you are completely satisfied with your book hook after the first attempt, but the work you put in on Day 1 will make Days 2–5 easier, and vice-versa. (Honestly, if you are happy with your book hook after one try, you need to get a second opinion.) Don't get hung up on polishing each day's assignment before proceeding.

Remember, your book proposal is a living document, not a static one. It should and will improve over time.

Let's get started on Day 2 by continuing with the Content section.

Premise

In some ways, your premise is an extension of your book hook. If you're writing a novel, your premise should describe in a few sentences more about the setting of the story, who your protagonist is, and the dilemma he or she is about to face.

If you're writing a nonfiction book, your premise should expand on why your book matters to the reader and how you and your book can guide the reader toward a resolution of his or her problem. Again, your premise should be only a few sentences longer than your book hook. The temptation here is to launch into a summary of your book, but don't do it. Instead, use this space to answer the following question: *What is the problem my book is addressing?* This is the place to address the pain your reader is facing.

Benefits

Benefits are what the reader will get from reading your book. The benefits are the solutions you offer to the problems you identified in your premise. When thinking of the benefits of your book, it is sometimes helpful to complete this sentence: *After reading the book, readers will....*

Following is a list of benefits taken from an agent's proposal for a book by an author with more than one million social media followers. After reading the book, readers will:

- Gain the courage to really connect with God and others
- Understand the importance of making time for quiet reflection
- Learn to live with less fear and more freedom
- Have a deeper sense of their own value and purpose
- Be equipped to have honest conversations about their struggles, questions, fears, and dreams

You'll notice that each benefit statement starts with a verb: *gain, understand, learn, have, be.* It's not required that your bullet points begin with a verb, but it's a good way to show that your book can make a real difference in readers' lives. Here are a few more good action verbs you can utilize: *create, find, rediscover, recognize, acquire, make, organize, transform.*

Pro Tip:
Keep your benefits statements brief—no more than four or five short bullet points. Make each statement powerful and believable.

Features

These are characteristics or qualities that make the book attractive to a prospective reader. In other words, features are things that will help the publisher and retailers to sell the book. There are primarily three types of features to consider: context features, content features, and author features.

Context features have to do with the cultural context into which your book is speaking. Perhaps your book addresses current events or a burning issue of our time. An unfortunate example of a context feature for a parenting book might be "Seven conversation starters to talk to your kids about school shootings."

Or maybe your book is timed to coincide with a major motion picture release or a significant anniversary of an important historical event. An example for your WWII historical novel might be:

Working Title releases simultaneously with the DVD of Best Picture Oscar nominee *Darkest Hour,* which has created renewed interest in World War II historical drama.

Content features of a book may include study questions for group discussion, photographs, journaling pages, or physical features such as a special binding or ribbon marker. Attributes of physical features will be dealt with later in the packaging section of your book proposal, but if a physical feature of the book is central to the concept, it's a good idea to include it here. An example of a content feature for a home improvement book might be "32 full-color photos illustrating the best life hacks for organizing your home."

Author features are things that make you uniquely positioned to write the book and reach your audience. Again, these will be covered in greater detail later in the proposal, but calling out one or two facts in this section is a good idea. For example, if you're uniquely qualified to write a book for schoolteachers, you might say, "With more than twenty-five years of classroom experience, Ann Q. Author speaks to more than a thousand teachers annually through in-service meetings, workshops, and regional education conferences."

If you can identify one or two bullet points each for context, content, and author features, you'll have a nice list.

Overview

The overview is a summary of your book, but it's also more. A good overview deals with the structure of the book. What you are really communicating to an agent or editor through this section is that you understand how a good book is organized and that your book will be structurally sound.

For a novel or narrative nonfiction, your book will likely be organized according to a story arc. For example, "Chapters 1–3 introduce the reader to young Teddy Roosevelt and the childhood illness that formed the foundation for his lifelong devotion to physical fitness," etc. For a how-to book, the book might be organized according to the steps in a process. For a daily devotional, the organizational principle might be a series of monthly themes.

Pro tip:
Be ready with a clear answer to the question, "How is your book structured?"

Whatever kind of book you're writing, it is critically important that you give serious thought to how it will be organized. You have likely already done so while outlining your book during the writing process. But it's a serious red flag for agents and publishers when an author fumbles with an answer to the question "How is your book structured?"

Chapter Titles

This is as simple as it sounds. It's a list of chapter titles you've developed for your book. If you've written a novel with numbered, untitled chapters, you can delete this section, especially if you've already provided a well-written overview. If yours is a nonfiction book, you are well advised to spend time developing your chapter titles. Excellent chapter titles can do a lot to draw readers into your book. If a potential reader is browsing books and your cover copy does its job, causing the customer (or agent or editor) to open the book and look inside, that person is likely to look at your table of contents and/or skim the chapter titles to find out what is covered in the book.

You don't need great chapter titles to write a good book proposal, but it helps. Nevertheless, don't allow yourself to get hung up on this section. If you have working chapter titles, plug them in for now, knowing that you will likely improve them over time.

Ancillary Products

Are there other products that might be produced to support your book or that could be derived from it? Common examples of ancillary products include a workbook, journal, daily reader, or calendar.

Pro Tip:

Listing several, unrealistic ideas for ancillary products may communicate to a publisher that you are distracted by dreams of bestseller status or that you think too highly of your work.

Be cautious about listing ancillary products. In most cases, it is better to allow an agent or editor to suggest a companion workbook. It's likely best to delete this section altogether unless there's an ancillary product that is central to the concept of your book.

The Manuscript

In this section of the proposal you will provide specific details regarding the length of your manuscript, where you are in the process of writing it, and how soon the publisher can expect to receive your completed manuscript.

Anticipated Manuscript Length

Estimate the final word count for your finished manuscript and round to the nearest thousand or five thousand. This is one of the few places in a book proposal where being less specific appears more professional. Even if your manuscript is finished, it's better to submit your proposal with an antici-pated length of 50,000 words than to write 48,347. The reason is that no matter who you are, your manuscript needs to be edited; more than likely you will end up with fewer (though sometimes more) words than in the "final" manuscript you turn in.

The important thing here is to try to be accurate within a couple thousand words. If your proposal says 50,000 words and you deliver 70,000, you are creating a whole lot of extra work for the editorial team. If you say 50,000 and deliver 30,000, you will likely be asked to go back and keep writing. In either case, you are causing delays that can disrupt an entire publishing cycle and create headaches for editorial, produc-tion, marketing, and sales. Delivering a manuscript that is well out of range of your anticipated word count will not win you friends inside the publishing house, where you need all the friends you can get.

That said, don't sweat your estimate too much. It's nearly impossible to estimate a word count precisely if you're still at the idea stage or in the early stages of writing. If that's you, try this: close your eyes and imagine someone sitting down to read your book. What size is it—small, average, oversized? How thick is the book? What do the pages look like? Are the pages readable and flowing and laid out like a novel for clean, easy reading? Are the pages spacious and gift-y with call-out quotes and design flourishes? Find a book on your bookshelf that is similar to what you're envisioning, and count the words on an average page. Multiply the total by the number of pages and round to the nearest thousand. You now have a reasonable target word count for your own book!

Anticipated Manuscript Completion Date

If you've already written your book, "The manuscript is complete" is always a wonderful sentence for an agent or reader to read. If you're still in process, then estimate a date when you expect to finish the book, typically the first day of a given month.

On many proposals represented by agents, you will see a phrase such as "Three months after contract signing." That is a power play that you probably should not attempt if you're an unknown author, especially if you're not represented by an agent.

Pro Tip:

Be realistic when estimating your manuscript completion date. Nothing gets an author-publisher relationship started on the wrong foot quite like a late manuscript. It's far better to under-promise and over-deliver.

Manuscript Status

If your manuscript is not yet finished, try answering this question as a percentage, such as "70% complete." Or you can express the status of your manuscript in terms of the projected word count—for example, "30,000 words are written of an eventual 80,000 total." The important thing is that your manuscript status and completion date be believable. In other words, give yourself more than two weeks to write 50,000 words.

Special Features

This section deals primarily with any features that will affect the page count, production time, or the cost of publishing the book. Examples of special features may be four-color printing, lined pages for journaling, an index of key terms or Bible references, a ribbon marker, or a sixteen-page photo insert with twenty-eight full-color photos.

Pro tip:
When including photos and illustrations, provide an exact number. Saying "53 color photos" is better than estimating "more than 50 photos." Not only will the publisher need this number to estimate printing costs, but the exact number will be included in the metadata sent to distributors.

Ultimately, the viability of including such features will be decided by the publisher, but including physical features in your proposal is important for sharing your vision. If you are working on a cookbook, for example, it's helpful for the publisher to know if you're thinking of a paperback with four-color pages and a lay-flat binding or spiral binding with pocket folders to hold handwritten recipes. Again, the final decision may not be yours to make, but it is reassuring to agents and editors to know you've put thought into it.

Even if you choose to publish independently in order to get exactly the book you're envisioning, you need to consider just how much the features you want will add to your printing and manufacturing costs.

The Package

In this section you'll provide the publisher with ideas you have for what your book will look like on the outside. While it's true that the graphics and text on the front and back covers will be designed by the publisher, you can use this section to help an agent or editor catch your vision for the book and communicate that vision to others during the critical decision stage that will ultimately determine whether or not you're offered a contract.

Preliminary Cover Concept

If you have an idea about what you'd like to see on the cover of your book, this is an opportunity to express it. However, keep it brief and don't be too specific.

While not directly germane to your book proposal, allow me to offer you some bonus advice on how to work with professional book designers. First, if you're publishing independently, hire an experienced professional designer and not your nephew who uses Photoshop to touch up the family's holiday photos. Second, the key to being happy with your final book cover is to offer the designer your preconceived ideas with an open hand and then stand back and let the experienced professional do his or her work. Share your ideas for the cover as concepts, not as demands, and you will get a much better design in the end.

Professional book designers are creative problem solvers. If they understand the premise, benefits, and features of your book—which they will after reading your awesome book proposal—a good designer will strive to provide you with a striking, (perhaps even surprising) visual and typographical representation of your concepts.

Pro Tip:

Make sure the book cover can sell your book when it's displayed thumbnail size, which is how most people will see it online and in print marketing materials.

When providing feedback to your designer, try to get to the heart of the problem to be solved rather than suggesting solutions. Instead of saying, "Make the subtitle bigger," you might say, "Can you make the subtitle more readable?" The heart of the problem here is readability, and good designers know that changing the font size is only *one* possible way to solve a readability problem and that doing so may create other problems on the cover.

Allow your designer to do what he or she does best. There's a reason people earn college degrees in graphic design and go on to specialize in book design. Allow your designer to use his or her gifts without being shackled to a predetermined vision.

Preliminary Back Cover Copy

Copy is simply the marketing message on the back (or flaps) of your book. Within a few precious seconds, this message must catch and hold the interest of a potential reader and persuade him or her to purchase the book. Likewise, your proposal will have only a few minutes to catch and hold the attention of an agent or editor, who is looking to be swept away by your well-written back cover copy, book hook, and premise.

Understanding that your publisher will likely assign a professional copywriter to rewrite your preliminary back cover copy down the road, this is nevertheless your opportunity to write a good summary of your book that can be used to create important sales pitches, marketing copy, and media kits.

So how do you write good back cover copy? First of all, keep it brief. Your copy shouldn't be more than 200 words in length. Remember, you have only a few seconds to make the sale. Be sure your hook is central to your copy—after all, the hook is why people will want to buy your book. If you're writing a nonfiction book, address your target audience directly, maybe even using second-person pronouns, as in "This book will change *your* life" or "*Your* friends will thank *you* for reading this book."

In *Building a StoryBrand*, Donald Miller suggests that you think of the person reading the back cover of your book as the flawed hero of their own story and your book as their guide on a journey. Identify the problem your hero (the reader) faces, empathize with them, and give them hope. Remind them what failure will look like if they don't read your book and what success will look like when they do.

Here's an early draft of the back cover copy I developed

for this book that you're reading now. It's definitely a work in progress, but here's where I was at the time of this writing:

Congratulations! You've decided to write a book and pursue the dream of becoming a published author. It is a noble calling.

You may have discovered by now that writing a book is also hard work that takes a lot of time. How do you make time in your busy day to write, especially when you don't even know where to start? Even if your book is already in print, you may find yourself stuck and asking the question "Now what do I do?"

Look, I've been there. I've helped more than 4,000 authors get published over the last twenty-five years, including traditionally published authors, assisted self-published authors, fully independent authors, and even my own work. I know the dedication required to publish a book, and I have good news:

You can get it done!

Complete Your Book Proposal in 5 Days guides you step by step through writing a book proposal and creating a plan for your ideas to take shape. This book will set you free to get the most out of the time you put toward your writing. *Complete Your Book Proposal in 5 Days* will help you organize your thoughts and plans around the three most important elements of publishing: your reader, your message, and your reach.

Your book proposal is the business plan for your book that will help you communicate effectively with agents, publishers, and the media. Best of all, a complete book proposal will give you confidence and clear steps to successfully publish your book.

A copywriter I am not.

It's a vulnerable thing to show your work to someone else, isn't it? I feel vulnerable about sharing this draft with you now, but I'm going to refine it over time and ask a couple of my copywriter friends to give me feedback. Feedback is an important part of the process of writing a book proposal too.

I strongly encourage you to join the community of authors and publishing industry experts at AuthorGateway.com. The people in the Author Gateway community support one another. They ask and answer each other's questions. They willingly share their book hooks and book covers, looking for feedback. It's an engaged group where you can readily get and give help, wherever you are on the path to publishing.

Day 2 Homework Assignment

You have some thought-filled work to do today. Drill deep into the social, emotional, and spiritual context in which you are writing your book. It is there that you will encounter the problems your readers commonly face. Spend time there while developing your premise. Your benefits and features will flow naturally from it. Your book hook is likely to get better because of it, and then you'll be well on your way to writing good back cover copy. If the structure of your book calls for chapter titles, spend some time today developing them to connect immediately with potential readers.

Remember to take deep breaths and just write. Give yourself permission to stop if you feel stuck.

Great job again today.

Day 3

You're doing great! You have what it takes to be a professional author: we're two days into the process, and you are persisting. Let's keep working our way through the proposal.

The Market

This section of the proposal is about clearly identifying the market for your book. Perhaps the most difficult part of defining your audience is fighting the temptation to think you've written a book that will appeal to everyone and anyone. While it seems counterintuitive to limit your potential readership to a single niche demographic, it is far more useful—and ultimately valuable—to identify a well-defined audience that wants and needs your book.

Pro tip:

A book for "everyone" is a book for no one.

Yes, your book, if published, will certainly draw some readers from outside your target market. But before a publisher commits precious financial and human resources to developing and promoting your book, they'll want to know there's a clear, identifiable target they can reach. They know that the more your book's content and marketing are aimed toward a specific consumer group, the more likely they are to hit the target and sell the book in large quantities. If you insist that your market is "All adults 18 and over," your efforts to reach that massive audience will be spread so thin that they will likely go unnoticed.

In some cases, such as children's books or gift books, it is useful to identify both a target reader and a target consumer. Ask yourself, "Who is my reader?" *and* "Who is my customer?" The reader and the customer are not always one and the same, and neither are the marketing tactics for reaching two different groups.

Keep in mind that your book hook and back cover copy should be addressed to the target reader rather than the target consumer. Take for example a devotional written for teens. While your customer may be a mom who buys the book for her teenage daughter, the cover needs to speak to the heart of the teenage daughter if you want her to read it.

However, for the purposes of completing the "Market" section of your book proposal, your focus and data must be aimed at the customer—the person who is going to purchase your book.

Characteristics

Complete this sentence: *The target audience for this book is made up of* _____.

Here you will specify the physical demographics of your customer. First, create a picture in your mind of the specific person who is going to buy your book. What is their gender? (Hint: women buy more books than men do.) How old is that person? You will need to express your target customer's age in terms of an age range. Common ranges include ages 4–8, 9–12, 13–17, 18–24, 25–34, 35–44, 45–54, 55–64, and 65+. "Baby/ toddler" is fine if you're writing a book for parents to read to very young children.

If your target reader and target customer are different, identify both but focus your primary attention on the customer in this section of the proposal.

Motivations

Why is your target customer going to buy your book? What needs do they feel that you can help meet? What pain do they suffer that you can help assuage? What feelings are they experiencing that you can validate? Your ability (or inability) to connect with the motivation of the person who buys your book may be the single most important factor in deciding your book's commercial destiny.

Fortunately, you've spent a good deal of time already thinking about these questions as you've been developing your book hook, premise, benefits, and features, so you this section may be a snap for you. On the other hand, if you've struggled with those sections earlier, this is a good time to camp out on this topic and really dig into it. The work you do here can help you to update and improve those earlier sections.

In *Building a StoryBrand*, Miller uses the language of a "problem." As yourself, *What is the problem my hero (the target customer) is facing in his or her own story?* Miller advises breaking this problem down into three layers: *external, internal*, and *philosophical*. Breaking down the customer's problem in this manner is how you will connect with them at a visceral level that cuts right to their motivation to buy your book. For the hero of this book, for example, the *external* problem is the need to get their book published. The *internal* problem is the confusion of not knowing where to start. The *philosophical* problem is the hero questioning whether he/she has what it takes. (You do!)

Another way to address motivations is to specifically identify the felt needs of the reader in his or her own voice, the emotions they're feeling, and the promise the book delivers. Here are three good examples from proposals developed by acquisitions editors for the Nelson Books imprint at HarperCollins Christian:

Example 1.

NEED: I feel discouraged and stuck. I need someone to show me how to overcome my current circumstances and begin to live with purpose and meaning again.

EMOTIONS:
- Discouraged
- Disappointed
- Hopeful

PROMISE: You can find new meaning and purpose in your life and become a part of God's bigger story.

Example 2.

NEED: I'm overwhelmed by the pressure to be constantly moving, always hustling, and continually achieving. I need a practical guide for my life that's realistic, doable, and gives me a fresh perspective.

EMOTIONS:
- Overwhelmed
- Anxious
- Exhausted
- Hopeful
- Eager

PROMISE: You will find practical tips and relatable advice for achieving meaningful goals in your life without feeling like you're better or worse than anyone else.

Example 3.
NEED: Sometimes life can feel so hard and overwhelming. I need to be inspired by a person who can stubbornly pursue joy and find it in small and simple things.

EMOTIONS:
- Hopeful
- Lost
- Uncertain

PROMISE: You can be inspired by this story and learn to see the potential of what God is doing right where you are.

Whether you address your customer's motivations to purchase your book in a narrative format or in a bulleted list as in these examples is completely up to you. What's important is recognizing that people buy books because they feel a real need at an emotional level. It's possible your customer hasn't fully identified their own feelings or emotions, but they will know when you connect with them at that level.

The importance of relentlessly pursuing the answer to the question "Why will my customer will buy this book?" cannot be overemphasized. It's not just a matter of making the sale. If you can't connect with your customer at an emotional level regarding their motivations, a reader is unlikely to connect with your book at all.

Identifying motivations is another way to home in on your specific target customer. Remember, a specific target is far more valuable than a broad, general market because it is reachable. A woman, age thirty-five to fifty-four, who actively volunteers at school and is terrified that her teenage daughter's self-esteem is being destroyed by social media, is much more reachable and motivated to find the solution to her specific problem than the broader group of "Women 35+ with children."

Affinity Groups

Now that you've identified your target market and considered their needs, emotions, and motivations, it will be easier to identify your customers' common interests. How do your target customers self-identify? Where do they tend to gather? To help get your wheels turning, here are several examples of well-known affinity groups: Mothers of Preschoolers (MOPS), the National Rifle Association (NRA), the National Association of Christian Counselors (NACC), Boy Scouts of America, the World Wildlife Federation, Mothers Against Drunk Driving (MADD), DivorceCare, and Facebook fan groups.

A good list of affinity groups will likely have some overlap with one another. After all, some affinity groups have millions of members. An important consideration before identifying an affinity group in your book proposal is the sense of identity that comes with being a member of that group. For example, the Automobile Association of America (AAA) is a massive group, but there's not as much sense of identity or emotion connected with being a AAA member compared to being an NRA member.

In the context of marketing your book, the most important factor for identifying a strong affinity group is its connection to your target market. An affinity group doesn't need to have millions of members to be influential, so drill down to consider smaller groups too. The best groups are the ones you can reach.

That said, when compiling your list, it's not a bad idea to include a group that has millions of members. Even if you don't have direct access to the group, chances are they publish a member magazine or e-newsletter, and that makes the group a publicity target. Present your list in your proposal in order from largest to smallest and include a note about any group that you can reach directly or indirectly.

Competitive Landscape and Differentiation

Where does your book fit in the current marketplace? What's being discussed in the media related to the topics covered in your book? Again, you've done some of this work already when doing research for the premise and features of your book. Search the Internet to find compelling, *recent* articles (within the past twelve months) from reputable sources. When citing an article in this section, include the source and the date it was published and write a couple sentences that show how the article demonstrates a high degree of public interest in the subject of your book and a hearty appetite for more information on the topic.

Pro tip:

Saying "There are no books like mine" is a dead giveaway that you're uninformed about the marketplace and haven't done your research. Don't use this phrase or anything close to it.

Don't be afraid of a little competition. If you think no one has written a book quite like yours, you haven't looked hard enough. The Harry Potter books were not the first published stories about boys and girls who attend magic school. Ursula K. Le Guin's *A Wizard of Earthsea* (1968), and Jill Murphy's *The Worst Witch* (1974), and Terry Pratchett's Discworld series are just a few of the works that have explored this terrain before J. K. Rowling took pen to paper. It's a good thing to have competition, especially books that were successful. That means there's a market for your subject.

This section of your proposal is an opportunity to differentiate your book from the competition. What are the top five bestselling books in your BISAC category? What did those books do that worked, and how does your book do that too? What did those books do that *did not* work, and how does your book do things differently? How does your book cover similar ground but go a step further than the competition?

Pro tip:
   **Resist the temptation to call your book the next
   _____ (fill in the title of an all-time
bestseller).**

The fact that *The Five Love Languages*, for example, is still in the top ten of *The New York Times* bestseller list of advice books more than two decades since it released is a testament to readers' perennial need to understand love relationships. It's not a bad idea to write a book on relationships and, in your proposal, point to a bestseller that demonstrates the public's appetite for your topic. However, you will come across as a crackpot if you claim that your book is the next *Five Love Languages*. Instead, work it into your copy that a perennial bestseller like *The Five Love Languages* demonstrates an ever-present need in the marketplace for good advice in this area of readers' lives.

Leave further comparisons to someone else. Don't make yourself look foolish and self-indulgent by saying, "If you like *The Five Love Languages*, you're going to love *My Working Title!*" or "*My Working Title* is Harry Potter meets *The Five Love Languages*." Don't create any opportunity for an agent or editor to roll his or her eyes while reading your proposal.

Comparative Sales Analysis

As we've seen with other parts of the book proposal, it may seem counterintuitive to give a shout-out to existing books that are most like yours, but doing so provides immediate insight and saves work for agents and editors who may be interested in your book.

Here's a peek behind the curtain at what happens inside a traditional publishing house. When an acquisitions editor sees enough merit in your proposal to take it to the publishing board (aka the pub board) for consideration, due diligence requires that the acquisitions editor research the sales of comparable titles to support his or her assumptions about where your book fits in the marketplace and how many copies it will sell. When you provide a list of comparable titles, including the basic metadata of those books, you are saving the editor time—and we all could use more time.

Keep in mind that the previous section dealing with Competitive Landscape should be presented in a narrative format; the Comparative Sales Analysis should be presented as a list. Go to the Resources section on AuthorGateway.com to download a free template used internally at HarperCollins Christian Publishing for comparative title analysis. As you will see, there are column headings for Title, Author, Release Date, Format, Price, Page Count, Trim Size, BISAC Code, Amazon Rank, and Date (of the reported ranking). This research takes considerable time to compile, but when an agent or editor sees that you have done 95 percent of the research, that says a lot to them about how easy it will be to work with you.

The other five percent of the research involves finding information that is likely outside your reach. This includes the Bookscan unit sales number and the agent's sales number. Bookscan is an industry sales reporting tool owned by Nielsen, the company best known for compiling TV show ratings. Bookscan data is not publicly available, nor is it affordable. This information is available only by corporate subscription and kept under strict license.

Bookscan captures a sizeable segment of actual cash register sales of books. However, because the Bookscan number represents only a portion of a book's total sales, this number is primarily used for benchmarking. Often a book will sell two or three times as many copies through channels that are not captured by Nielsen, hence the column for the agent's sales number.

Day 3 Homework Assignment

Research. Spend some additional time developing your premise and context features into copy about the competitive landscape. Don't be afraid of your competition. Instead, hunt them down. I worked for a publisher whose rule of thumb for acquiring new books was that a book had to steal someone's place among the top three titles in the category. If she didn't believe the book could become a top-three bestseller in its category, she didn't want to invest in it. Have all of her books hit top-three status? Rarely, but she is dogged about research. Data backs up every decision she makes, but she also has incredible instincts and a heart for great stories. Do as much research as you can and develop the story about why your book deserves its place as a top-three bestseller in its category.

Your other assignment for today is to get some rest, because we're going deep on Day 4 into the realm of who you are and how you will market your book. You will be amazed at everything you're capable of doing once you spend time developing a plan.

You're doing a great job. Keep persisting. Your hard work will pay off.

Day 4

You've done so much great work the past three days identifying the context for your book, your specific audience and the pain they feel, and the benefits your book offers to guide them toward the resolution they desire. Today you will work through the remaining sections of the book proposal template, so let's keep moving.

The Author

This section of the proposal is focused primarily on you, the author. Selling oneself does not come naturally to many of us. It might even feel a little icky, especially in those terms. Yet if you're going to be an author engaged in the business of publishing, you need to work through your reservations until you come to a place where you are comfortable being the expert on your book and confident talking about why *you* are qualified to write it.

Author Background

Try writing your background as though you're preparing for a job interview. You're expected to bring a certain confidence into an interview. I once heard a podcast on preparing for the common job interview icebreaker "Tell me about yourself." The podcaster encouraged listeners to develop a three-to-four-minute response in which everything you share communicates something about your goals, accomplishments, and key lessons you've learned in a way that will be relevant and attractive to a prospective employer. I encourage you to apply this same philosophy to drafting your biography.

Your background should be more than a series of mere facts. Tell a story about yourself, with a running thread that shows how the events in your life led up to your writing this book.

Pro Tip:
Tell your story, but keep every fact relevant to your book.

When considering what qualifies someone to write a book, it's common to think of the letters that follow someone's name and represent their various degrees and certifications (Phd, MDiv, CPA, JD, etc.). Whether or not you have a bunch of fancy letters after your name, your personal story is full of events that have pointed you toward writing your book. But how do you know which of these events and/or qualifications are relevant to your book proposal and which are not?

If you've written a book on parenting teens and you're a licensed marriage and family counselor, your academic and professional training should definitely be part of the story you tell in your proposal. On the other hand, if you're a dentist and you've written a novel set during the Civil War, listing "DDS" after your name on the book cover is not particularly helpful, nor is it recommended. What's more important to your story is the paper you wrote in fifth grade about the Battle of Gettysburg. The paper itself is not as important as your interest in the Civil War and the fact that you've been researching it since grade school. While this fact is not itself bullet-point worthy, it does show that you've been preparing most of your life to write this book. All the time you've spent pursuing this interest by visiting battlefields and museums, reading histories, and watching documentaries on the war is, in part, what led you to write your book. You want to phrase all of it in professional terms, of course, but the research born out of your personal interest may be what qualifies you to write on this topic. (Note that it's the research on the subject that qualifies you, not your personal interest in and of itself.)

If you've written a book for parents on helping children overcome an eating disorder because you walked that road yourself, your ability to connect with readers at an emotional level because of the pain you've experienced may be what qualifies you to write your book. However, in most cases of writing on clinical topics (e.g., surviving cancer or overcoming agoraphobia), you should consider asking someone with a clinical degree to coauthor the book with you to reinforce its credibility with a publisher and in the marketplace. If coauthorship isn't possible or practical, try getting a foreword written by a PhD, MD, or other professional. Multiple endorsements from professionals in the field can also reassure readers that your advice is sound.

Your background statement is going to include "why" you wrote your book, but don't dwell there unnecessarily. If your reasons for writing the book connect with the motivations of your target customer to buy your book, then it is worthy of exploring more deeply. Otherwise, an agent or an editor is far more interested in your target customer's motivations to buy the book than in your motivations to write it.

As you tell your story, consider sharing the names of cities where you've lived, companies where you've worked, and other personal details that might trigger ideas for promotions and bulk sales opportunities. If you're willing to put in the legwork, you could potentially get your book stocked in the "Local Author" section of bookstores in every city where you've lived.

Allow yourself to wander mentally as you write about everything that has influenced you to write your book. Once you've rediscovered the life experiences that brought you to this point, refine them into a professional narrative that reveals your goals, accomplishments, and the key lessons that prepared you to write this book. But remember, this is a book proposal, not your autobiography. As with a three-to-four-minute answer in a job interview, keep it short and moving. Tell your story in less than 500 words—and in third person— to make a professional impression on an editor or agent.

Book Bio

As with your background, your book bio should be written in third person. The difference between your background and your book bio is the length and the intended audience. Your background will be read by agents, editors, and marketing pros who are looking for angles to help them develop your book and promote it. Your book bio should be written to the potential customer who's looking at the back cover to find out who you are.

The book bio should be very brief—around fifty words.

Include only those facts relevant to the book. Here's a working draft of my book bio for this book:

> Paul Mikos is a successful publishing professional with more than twenty years' experience in the book business. He's helped publish more than 4,000 books in his career and has a passion to help authors find fulfillment in book publishing.

It needs work, but as I refine it I will make sure I'm hitting the right points and not being redundant.

Published Books

In the Comparative Sales Analysis spreadsheet that you downloaded as part of Day 3's assignment, you will notice another tab for "Author's Previous Books." The sheet includes the same columns for title data with some additional columns for sales reporting. If you've published one or more books already, as the author this data should be readily available to you. If you haven't published any previous books, delete this section.

Other Published Writing

List any articles you've written, including the title of the article, name of the publication or website, date of publication, and the circulation or number of followers (if you can get those numbers).

It's important to strike a good balance when reporting other published writing. You want to demonstrate that you've written work others have deemed worthy of publishing. On the other hand, you may not want to include *everything* you've written. Stay on topic and list only those pieces that are relevant to the general subject area of your book. The exception would be if you wrote an off-topic piece that was published in a high-profile publication. Be intentional and strategic with what you share, just as you would in your résumé when applying for a job.

Marketing and Promotion

Writing an outline of the basic marketing actions *you* will take to promote your book is the start of putting together a great marketing plan. While writing a complete marketing plan is something every author should do, it is beyond the scope of this book. The goal for this section of your book proposal is simply to outline a plan and capture the highlights of the creative things you will do to market yourself and your book. We will spend more concentrated time exploring an author's marketing opportunities on Day 5.

Platform

A platform is the number one thing that gets an author past the gatekeepers in order to achieve the Holy Grail: a book publishing deal. Your platform refers to the scope of opportunities you have to influence people in your target market.

If you currently have tens of thousands of social media followers, you have a platform worth noting in this section. If you speak publicly at events attended by thousands of people annually, you have a platform. If you run a company or nonprofit with thousands of employees and/or supporters, you have a platform. If you have a website or blog with thousands of unique visitors every month, or you host a weekly podcast with thousands of regular listeners, you have a platform.

For most of us, however, this is simply not the case. If you do not have an impressive platform, you should delete this section and focus instead on the "Personal Marketing and Promotion" section. This is NOT permission, however, to give up on marketing your book. In fact, quite the opposite is true. While you may not have a platform that reaches thousands, begin with the few dozen people you do know and begin building from there.

Michael Hyatt is the author of the book *Platform: Get Noticed in a Noisy World—A Step-by-Step Guide for Anyone with Something to Say or Sell.* As a former publisher and CEO of Thomas Nelson Publishers, Mike understands writers and is a bestselling author himself. His book is an excellent guide to building your platform, and I highly recommend that every new or unknown author read it.

Personal Marketing and Promotion

This is where you'll provide a thorough outline of your planned personal activities in support of your book. Many of the same items mentioned in the "Platform" section—social media, speaking engagements, online marketing—should be included here. Such activities are critically important to the commercial viability of your book, but they also add to the personal fulfillment you'll experience as a published author.

On Day 5, we will discuss a number of options for expanding your platform that might be within your reach and will demonstrate to an agent or publisher that you've got the drive and willingness to help sell your book. To get a head start on Day 5, you may want to jot down a few marketing ideas now that you can return to tomorrow.

Marketing and Promotion

This is where you will outline any paid advertising and earned media (i.e., publicity gained through promotional efforts other than paid advertising) that you're prepared to contribute in support of your book, usually at a national level.

Maybe you have some cool ideas for promoting your book, such as developing a companion mobile app. However, if you're not planning to pay for these promotional tools yourself, just delete this section from your proposal. Your publisher will decide how much budget they want to allocate toward marketing your book and how they will spend it.

For example, if you're investing your own money to hire a marketing agency or publicist, you will want to list the company or individual you are engaging, the scope of work you've hired them to do, and the amount (budget) you plan to spend. If an agent or publisher sees that you're willing to spend $10,000 of your own money on marketing, they may be willing to advise you on how to get the most for your money.

Paid marketing includes things such as Google AdWords, Facebook advertising, and other paid ad placements. Many companies and websites—especially Facebook—will entice you to spend just $20 to try advertising with them. But while it's thrilling to "boost" a post for $20 and see that it got a thousand views, that only means that a thousand people scrolled past your post in their Facebook news feed.

Before you spend any of your own money on paid advertising, I suggest you get some training. Author Gateway offers courses on effectively using social media, and there are plenty of other online courses and podcasts available on similar topics. Generally, however, if you're going to spend your own money on paid advertising, it's a good idea to hire a professional with book marketing experience who can report defined, quantifiable results of your expenditures.

Earned media refers to publicity coverage in national and high-profile regional news and entertainment media. (This category does not include neighborhood newspapers and alumni newsletters; those can be included under "Personal Marketing and Promotion.") Earned media is often considered to be "free" simply because you can't pay to get this kind of coverage, and that's true by definition. However, writing effective press releases to generate coverage in national media often requires expertise that only comes at the price of hiring an expert publicist. Media producers and news editors know which publicists bring them the best stories, just as publishers know which agents bring them the best books. So while media coverage is technically "free," gaining access to that media can be expensive. And don't forget the cost of printing and mailing advanced reader copies of your book to solicit reviews.

If you plan to hire a publicist, do your research. Find a publicist who has a track record of getting media coverage and reviews for books like yours. Again, you should only list a publicist or agency in this section if you are planning to hire and pay them yourself. Should you get a traditional book deal, your publisher will most likely assign a staff publicist to work with you.

If you have experience writing press releases, you may include that in this section. It's important, however, that you truly understand what is newsworthy and how to write effective headlines. Again, there is training available to learn how to do this. Otherwise, it's best to leave it to the professionals.

Ancillary Materials Available

List any ancillary materials that you're including with the proposal. For example, you might attach a chapter-by-chapter synopsis of your book, two or three sample chapters, and maybe sample illustrations, if illustrations are a key element of your book.

This is a great place to provide links to videos of you speaking at an event or in the media, or audio of you appearing on a radio program or podcast. Even if the topic you're addressing in the audio/video is not especially relevant to your book, media samples allow an agent or publisher to get an idea of what they can expect when they arrange a media appearance for you.

Day 4 Homework Assignment

Spend time writing up your background and editing it into a job-interview-worthy pitch about who you are and why you're qualified to write your book. Tell your story in a personal way and connect with your reader on a human level. While telling your story, stay professional and write in the third person. Remember, the reader of your background is the industry professional who's interested not only in your qualifications, but also any marketing opportunities that come out of your background.

Be honest with yourself about your platform and your willingness to build it. Get a copy of Michael Hyatt's book *Platform: Get Noticed in a Noisy World* and begin thinking about how you will start building and expanding your sphere of influence.

Great job today. You're almost there.

Day 5

An author's ability and willingness to market his or her own book is critically important to getting a book deal. (It's even more important if publishing independently.) Today we will look at several marketing opportunities that are within your reach and perhaps spur some new ideas for self-promotion that you haven't yet considered. You may not feel qualified to market your book, or maybe you just don't know where to start. That's why we're dedicating this day to developing the marketing section of your book proposal.

Believe this: marketing is something you *can* do. In fact, it's something you *must* do, whether you publish independently or sign with a traditional publisher. The fact is no one can market a book like its author, and authors who demonstrate the ability and willingness to promote their book have a much better shot at landing an agent and a book deal. Agents and publishers want to work with authors who will proactively engage with customers. If you appear unwilling to participate in the marketing of your own book, you can just about give up on your dreams of signing a book deal.

Get SMART

Setting SMART goals is one key to having a fulfilling publishing experience. If you're not familiar with the concept, SMART stands for *specific, measurable, achievable, realistic,* and *timely.* Based on your SMART goals you can plan specific actions you will take, with measurable results you can realistically achieve. Making a plan with SMART goals allows you to operate with confidence, knowing just what steps you need to take next to achieve those goals.

Website and Blog

It's not too early to build your author website, and it makes a strong impression on agents and publishers to see www.yourname.com online. Maybe you're wondering if you should create a website that's about you, or one that's about your book. Generally, I suggest that you build an author-specific website with dedicated pages for your books. This kind of site can be expanded to promote future books.

Whether you already have a website or are just developing one, it's wise to consider how you will attract viewers to the site. This is one area where the book *Platform* can be helpful in developing the strategies and content you will use to build a following and compile a mailing list that allows you to stay in direct contact with your audience.

Of course, the idea of building a website can be intimidating. One web-building service I've found to be very user-friendly is Wix.com. Their automated system will ask you a series of questions and then build a site for you in minutes. The site has design themes and images you can choose from, or you can upload your own. The system will even create a logo for you, if you want. If you're comfortable navigating the Internet, you probably have enough skill to build a website using Wix. Of course, you can always hire a professional web designer to assist you in building your site.

Social Media

By virtue of owning a Facebook or Instagram account, you've already demonstrated a rudimentary understanding of managing social media. If you're not active on social media, let me assure you that you *can* learn it and begin to build a following.

Remember that most people are on Facebook for personal use only. One author expressed her frustration that she could post a picture of her dog in a sweater and get fifty likes in thirty seconds, but when she posted a link to her book there were only crickets. She was hurt that she couldn't get her friends and family to take an interest in her work, let alone strangers. This is a case in point as to why it's so important to know your target market. This case also demonstrates the need to understand best practices for marketing with social media, which is beyond the scope of this book. Research social media best practices and how and where to set up accounts and pages for you and your book.

Perhaps you are already following the Author Gateway page on Facebook and have joined in our group discussion. If not, I encourage you to do so as soon as possible. Also, Author Gateway's "Marketing Your Book" course includes an entire session dedicated to digital marketing, and we are developing another series dedicated to social media in which we will explore the topic more thoroughly.

Endorsements and Influencers

Endorsements lend you credibility as the author and speak to the quality of what you've written. Start by creating a list of people who A) have influence with your target market, B) you can reach through your personal network to ask them to endorse your book, and C) are likely to agree to do it.

If your book is nonfiction, a foreword by an *appropriate* individual might help sell more books. No one is going to care what your accountant, Bob, thinks of your history of NHL hockey, no matter how good he is with numbers. So whom should you ask to write your foreword? It's always a good idea to get someone who's an expert in the field you're writing about, especially a person whose credentials can be easily communicated along with their name on your cover.

A respected individual with well-known ties to your subject is also a strong choice. For example, retired four-star general and former Secretary of State Colin Powell may not be an expert on cancer, but he has fought prostate cancer and won and would be an excellent choice to write a foreword for your book on battling cancer. Of course, your foreword writer doesn't have to be a household name, as long as the person is well known to your target audience.

In addition to seeking endorsements or a foreword, you should also consider contacting people and organizations who can create bulk sales opportunities for your book. Do you know any corporate CEOs who might buy a few hundred copies of your book as a motivational tool for their employees? Do you know any ministries that might give your book away as gifts for their supporters or viewers? Or any financial supporters of the ministry who would pay for the books for the ministry to give away?

Speaking Schedule

Public speaking is a challenge for most of us, but it is one of the best things you can do to promote your book. Showing an agent or publisher that you are able and willing to speak publicly about your book is very influential when pursuing a book deal.

If you have an opportunity to speak directly to your target audience, it's best to schedule speaking engagements for when your book is available. Of course, any time you can get in front of people is an opportunity to become a better speaker and is especially valuable when you're just starting to build a platform. Many aspiring authors think their book will be the impetus to become a public speaker, yet establishing yourself as a speaker now can help you land a book deal.

Remember that becoming a published author gives you credibility, but it doesn't mean that speaking opportunities will just fall in your lap. It takes effort and gumption to book your first speaking engagements. The good news is there are many civic groups, historical societies, museums, corporations, libraries, senior centers, and other forums that welcome speakers, and each one represents an opportunity for you to promote yourself and sell your book.

Personal Networking

One way to mine for speaking opportunities is through personal networking. Join a local writer's group and make friends with other writers who may have helpful connections. Meetups are another great way to leverage the social power of the Internet to find and connect with people who have similar interests. Visit www.meetup.com and look for groups that meet in your area. You may or may not have an opportunity to present your book to a group, but you'll still be able to network and ask people for referrals to other groups.

Every time you talk about your book with an individual or group, one of the best things you can do is ask if they have any contacts who might be interested in your book and if they'd be willing to make an e-mail introduction. Generally, people want to help, and an e-mail introduction is a relatively easy thing to do. Always have your business card ready so you can ask someone to make an introduction for you. Your list of affinity groups is also a useful tool for networking. It's much easier for someone to look at a list and mention someone they know at one of the organizations. Or they may be able to suggest another useful organization you haven't yet considered.

Local Retail

Do the bookstores in your area have a "Local Author" section? Ask if they would be willing to include your book. Be liberal about what might be considered "local." Any bookstore within fifty miles (an arbitrary number) of your hometown counts. In fact, any bookstore within fifty miles of any town where you've ever lived would qualify. What matters to the retailer is if it will help the book sell. Once you have the book placed in stores, contact your personal network and ask people to purchase a copy to support the local bookshop and create a demand for your book.

You can check with local chain bookstores, but most will defer to the home office for buying decisions, which is a polite way of saying no. But sometimes a chain store manager can make buying decisions, and you may find that they're very supportive of local authors. Also consider talking to other retail shops that sell books—local gift shops, hospitals, churches, etc. Keep in mind, however, that purchasing for airport stores, grocery stores, drugstores, big box stores (e.g., Costco) is done almost exclusively at the corporate level, so you may not want to invest much time working that angle.

Put some effort into making relationships with local retailers. You can offer to do a book signing or give a talk and sign books afterward. Or plan a book party and ask your local bookstore to host it. An impressive bullet point in your book proposal is something like "Commitments from 17 local retailers to stock the book."

Print Collateral

There are a handful of promotional pieces that are worth printing and always keeping on hand:

- A business card with your book cover and contact info
- Bookmarks for giveaways at speaking gigs or to be used by bookstores as bag-stuffers
- "Signed by Author" stickers are a nice touch for a book in the "Local Author" section

Pro Tip:

If you sign books in advance, leave space above your signature to come back and personalize the copy later.

If you are marketing your book with such tools, it's worth including a sentence about it in the book proposal. If you are the kind of author who is handing out business cards and bookmarks, you're clearly an author who is willing to hustle. An agent or publisher is more likely to invest in you when they see you investing in yourself.

Putting It All Together

The "Personal Marketing and Promotion" section of your proposal doesn't need to be a full-blown marketing plan. Rather, this should be an outline of basic work you are doing and have scheduled to do once your book releases. Building a website, creating a social media footprint, and public speaking may be outside your comfort zone, but it doesn't mean these things are beyond your reach. Public speaking may not be physically or emotionally possible for you presently, but don't give up. You are a creative communicator. What are some other ways you can talk to your target audience? If you can't speak at a luncheon club, can you book yourself as a guest columnist for a monthly e-newsletter?

Set some SMART goals for the action steps you want to take. What's a realistic, achievable number of speaking gigs you could book over a three-month period? How many hours per week are you going to spend researching groups and calling activity coordinators? How many meetups will you attend in a month?

Conclusion

Congratulations! You made it through the five days and have completed a solid draft of your book proposal. You deserve to feel excited and proud of the work you've done. You now know more about the market, more about your book, and more about yourself than you did when you started.

Is Your Book Proposal Ready for Prime Time?

Over that last five days, we've walked section by section through the book proposal template. Now is a good time to circle back and use what you've learned this week to polish the fine points of your proposal. After researching the competitive landscape, do you feel confident about your title and subtitle, the trim size, and the price you've proposed for your book? Have you sharpened your book hook? Did you discover new features about your own book from reading the descriptive copy of your competitors? Did you gain some clarity or pick up new ideas for improving your book's structure or chapter titles?

While your book proposal will continue to guide you like a good business plan, you should continue to refine and update your proposal like you would a good résumé. Remember, the primary job of the book proposal is to get you a book deal.

Your book proposal is the single most important tool for opening doors with literary agents, acquisitions editors, booksellers, and even the media. It is the best representation of your book that industry professionals are likely to see before they ask to see more.

The 5-Day Challenge to Complete Your Book Proposal

Additional insights and encouragement to finish your book proposal are available through an online workshop, The 5-Day Challenge to Complete Your Book Proposal, hosted by Author Gateway. The workshop features videos with yours truly that follow the outline of this book and the Author Gateway Book Proposal Template. The videos provide more examples and stories and bring an interpersonal touch to help get you through the book proposal writing process. The workshop has received raving reviews from participating authors and is highly recommended as a companion for this book.

You may find it in the Resources section at www.AuthorGate way.com.

It's Time to Get Some Feedback

Author Gateway has assembled a community of people who care about one another and are helping each other. This community of writers is a great way to get feedback on your work and develop your network of contacts. Visit AuthorGateway.com to read more about us and follow the "Get Started" link to join our community. There's much to learn and even more to gain when you engage with others and share your work.

Ready to Find an Agent?

Author Gateway has compiled a list of more than sixty literary agents who are actively representing books by Christian authors. The list is available in the Resources section of AuthorGateway.com. The list includes the name of the agent, their agency's name, website address, mailing address, and e-mail address. You can start sending your book proposal out immediately!

Author Gateway also offers a three-day workshop on how to work with literary agents. In this workshop you will learn:

- The role of an agent and the benefits you'll receive from their expertise
- The strategic, legal, and financial advantages of working with a literary agent
- How to identify the best agents for you and your book
- What agents are looking for and how to grab their attention
- How to position your book and yourself as strongly as possible in a query letter
- How to improve your query or proposal to hire the agent you really want
- Critical success factors for landing the right agent and book deal
- Standard agency contract terms and appropriate financial relationships
- Questions to ask other writers before hiring an agent
- How to obtain the best information and training possible if you choose to self-publish

Visit the Resources section of AuthorGateway.com for more information on this valuable workshop.

Want a Professional Opinion before Sending Your Proposal?

If you'd like professional feedback on your book proposal before you start sending it to agents and publishers, Author Gateway offers a Book Proposal Critique Service. An experienced book publishing industry professional will read your proposal and provide a written evaluation with suggestions for improvements to help you avoid the pain and frustration that comes from submitting your proposal to agents and publishers before it is ready.

Really Need a Hand?

Perhaps the constraints on your time are too great to dedicate your full attention to developing a strong book proposal. For you, Author Gateway also provides a Book Proposal Development Service. An experienced book publishing industry professional will work with you directly to create your book proposal and prepare it to be submission-ready for sending to agents and publishers.

Still Much More to Come!

Author Gateway exists to help authors define success and achieve it. We are developing new resources and educational opportunities to help you with marketing, publicity, social media, and so much more. You can help us to develop the tools that are most useful and important to you by staying connected to our community of authors and industry professionals. Visit AuthorGateway.com and click the "Get Started" link today!

Congratulations on completing your book proposal!

Keep us posted on your success.

Email us anytime at hello@authorgateway.com.

CPSIA information can be obtained
at www.ICGtesting.com
Printed in the USA
LVHW012148200619
621914LV00005B/56/P

9 781400 325061